The Dragon
&
The Dragonfly

poems by
Carol Despeaux Fawcett

i

Photographs © by Cliff DesPeaux
Water Droplets on Maple Leaf p. 5, Neighbors p. 16, Italian Lights and Cross p. 19, Cabin Buried in Snow p. 40, Italian Cat on Bench p. 45, Italian Arches p. 69, Harrison Lake, Canada p. 76, Chipmunk on Mountain p. 82, Raccoon p. 88.

Photographs © by Carol Despeaux Fawcett
Dale and Ruby p. iv, Washington State Ferry p. 29, Italian Church on Rock p. 34, Water God Statue p. 61, Seabeck p. 93, Butterfly p. 95.

Mixed media butterfly art p. 13 © Bryn Hamano Hughes
Canoe in tree art p. 29 © Evy Olson Halvorsen
Green fruit avocado art p. 59 © Sydni Sterling

Front Cover art and interior dragonfly art
© by Carol J. Bankhead
Book design by Paula Gill

Published by Blue Dragonfly Press
ISBN-13: 978-0-692-98936-4
Printed in America

The man with the cat in his arms

is gone. The picture I carry was taken
on his birthday, 4 months before he left.
He's holding our orange cat with the white bib—
a vase of birthday flowers tucked in the crook of his elbow.
Two parrots—one blue, one red—pop out
of the painting on the wall behind him, as if perched
on his right shoulder. His smile is tired, peaceful.
His eyes say *thank you, I love you*. The cat looks confused,
ears splayed, not sure where she is
or where she is going.

We had just returned from brunch
at the Port Ludlow Inn where we sat
in front of a cheery fake fire, he reading
another book on spiritual awakening, me etching
another poem on paper. Or was it a short story?
And why can't I remember? Each detail—
what he wore, what I wrote, what we ate—
now necessary, like air or water
or warm bodies holding one another
in the darkest part of night.

Each detail is a small stone
I rub between my fingers, worrying
away life's edges, as if minutia matters,
as if life or death can be counted, can be quantified—
19 flowers, 2 birds, 1 cat, 1 man.
No. The counting is for the living.
1 day and 1 day and 1 day and then
it will be your birthday again.
The cat and I will be here
waiting.

Table of Contents

III. A New Vocabulary

IV. Lessons

V. When Love Comes

Walking Through Woods

I would love to live
Like a river flows,
Carried by the surprise
Of its own unfolding.

John O'Donohue, "Fluent"

Poulsbohemian Poetry Reading
for Everett Thompson

I arrive late, as usual, scan
the room for a place to sit.
Every chair full of poets
and poetry-lovers in spring
finery—purple scarf, red velvet
shawl, blonde beret, brown beret,
even a man in green corduroy.

Though it's only April, sweaty
air pushes me and my fresh grief
to the back of the room where I find
you, poet friend, leaning against a table.
The gray in your plaid shirt
matches the gray in your beard
like a flounder I once saw
that changed its color to blend
into the bottom of the sea.

I relax into the spaciousness
that seems to follow you—
no—"follow" is not the right word.
If I've learned anything from you,
it's the importance of choosing
the right word.

No *heart* or *soul* or *love*
but useful words like
wooden leg, trillium, gun.
Words that tell us where we come
from and who we are.

This night, I wonder how you would write me.
Would I be a broken chair, a rusted saw,
a faded painting that has spent too much
time in the sun?

I lean against the sturdy
wooden table, settle into
this quiet of a man
who knows his words.

I walk through woods

where rain pelts maple leaves
to the ground.

Beyond cries
of seagulls fighting over

broken clams, the constant
din of a carpenter's hammer

penetrates fog, binds sky to earth.
I wonder, does the workman love his work?

Does his face flush, do his palms
throb with the life he builds

for others? Will he go
home to a warm fire,

a woman wearing his flannel shirt,
a place he calls his own

made of wood and brick and ochre
dreams? Will any of us?

Catman and Spirit

He pulls on his boots, his rust-colored poncho,
slips on our favorite gray knapsack,
calls to me, "Come, Spirit. Time for a ride."

Knowing his words are true, that "ride"
is not euphemism for "vet," I hop from floor
to couch to top of knapsack where, over time,
my body has molded its shadow.

Through New Mexico, through Arizona
through Seattle, we've travelled and slept and loved.
We miss the red-haired waitress the most.
Each night she brought home new scents:
salmon, filet mignon, chicken marsala, crab.
She smelled of heaven. She smelled of home.

She died in my tenth year, the smells
not so good then. But today the sun rises,
we ride to the farmer's market.
Tall on my knapsack, gray fur catching wind,
I lift my nose to honeysuckle, cinnamon,
the sweaty sweetness of humans who wear

emotions like perfume—
fear, hope, loneliness, love.
I want to stay here forever.
Can't wait to go home.

Broken Things

Left on Rainsong, right on Roxbury, red
and white For Sale sign marks the drive.
"Everything cheap," says the middle-aged
woman in long flowered dress and Avon perfume.
"Divorcing. All must go. Cheap." Her sharp

Armenian accent slaps down words
like a game of 21. Shuffling through boxes,
I pull out a porcelain gravy boat, antique
china dolls. Her husband watches
from the garage. His hands twitch

like a man recently done with cigarettes.
She drops her voice as if telling a secret,
"Make offer. All must go."
"How much for this?" I point to a wooden
ladder with two broken rungs.

"Forty dollar," he says.
"Twenty," she counters, flashing ten fingers twice
as if I don't understand English or the language
of broken things. I give him thirty, rolled up
so she can't see, and drive the ladder home.

I offer it to my neighbor. Married for 40 years,
he's good at fixing things.

Advice from a Male Tasmanian Cave Spider

Spin gracefully. Feed on anything big enough or dumb
enough to jump, fly, or fall into your web. Don't be
a glutton. Save some for later, invite friends for a feast.

Create strong structures. Hang by your own thread.
Practice disjointedness whenever you can.
Save your venom for special occasions.

Perpetuate your mythos of mystery and doom.
Scuttle across cave ceilings. Lurk in darkness.
Spend time in your inner cave. Throw shadows

across the walls to scare scientists studying you
for their documentary. Haunt the author
of Coraline so he writes you into his next novel.

Cultivate a following. Flaunt your prehistoric nature.
Don't worry if smaller-minded relatives make fun of you.
They don't live decades, stretch the length of a dinner plate.

Develop a fondness for large-bellied females. Pluck
your web nightly to attract a mate. Knead her softly.
Spread her fangs apart so she can't kill you.

Remember, you have eight legs, but sixteen when
making love. Learn to embrace change in case one day
you find yourself squinting into the light.

Making Love on the Buddha

Ladybug crawls
across the stone god's lap. He's
faded from rain and wind
crumbling with age—
yellow crocuses adorn his feet.

Ladybug bows in seeming supplication,

fans her black lace wings.
Another bright body
lights atop her—
feels for the spot
that will set them free.

Assisted Living Questionnaire

1. Ruth Ann Rosenberg, 78.

2. Caucasian (with a bit of Russian, though sometimes I get mistaken for Irish—which is silly since my color, Terra-cotta red, is from a bottle).

3. Melanie Amster, daughter. 360-555-1212.
(I have a son but his born-again wife won't let him talk to me. He has to sneak-call me—so don't call them).

4. Medicaid.

5. No idea. Ask my daughter. She takes care of my money.

6. See above.

7. Answer to all is NO, except Angina and Arthritis— AA but I don't drink (much).

8. Sometimes farting. But only after I eat cabbage or beans.

9. Constipated—if I eat too much cheese or ostrich.

10. You're kidding, right? I'm too old to drive. Even if I did, I'd never own an STD—my son-in-law says they have a high rollover rate. And he should know.

11. None of your business.

12. No, never fainted. Came close once. Walked in on my son-in-law and daughter doing the horizontal tango on the dining room table. Never knew a man could have so much hair on his butt.

13. I don't smoke—except when I sleepwalk.

14. Two bottles of port (per week, not day). I hide it in

my underwear drawer from my grandson Dilbert.
I think his name is Dilbert. He acts like a Dilbert.

15. Yes

16. No, I've never wandered. Except that time I
slipped into Bud Larsen's place after his wife died and
gave him a good old-fashioned hand job in the middle
of the night. I put a pillow over his face so he wouldn't
know it was me. He quit struggling after awhile.

17. N/A

18. My memory's just fine, thank you very much.
Even remember what shoes I wore—brown penny
loafers—when we buried my ma. I remember how
the grave dirt stuck to my soles. How I quit wearing
those shoes after that. I didn't want the dirt to fall away.

19. Once. Western State Hospital. They say it was for
attempted suicide but that's hooey. I only took those
pills cuz I thought they were the kind that made you
horny. If I'd known they were going to make me believe
I was the reincarnation of Frida Kahlo and paint
my self-portrait across our town hall in the middle of
the day naked, I'd never have taken them.

20. None.

21. Good. But I'm no pig. Unlike our neighbor Mrs.
Whipple. That woman eats two dinners—one at 5pm
and one at 9pm. When her husband disappeared, I
told the policeman she probably sliced him up and ate
him. He just smirked and gave me that look that says
he thinks I'm crazy. But they never did find her husband.
Mark my words.

22. When you're older, time is precious. You don't waste it on bullshit.

23. I don't want my daughter to worry about me. If I'm not there, she won't worry so much. Out of sight, out of mind. She's got her own life, own kids. I can volunteer here—do something to keep myself busy—sell cookies or doilies. I can sell anything. Just don't ask me to make it. I quit cooking after Herb died.

24. Not even on Sundays.

25. Reading. Listening to music. I like all kinds but country. I mean, really—why sing about a cheating husband or your dog getting hit by a car? Life's tough enough without being reminded about it. Besides, country music makes you dumb. They got studies to prove it.

26. None of your business.

27. No. I'm not vegetarian, vegan, kosher, gluten-free, dairy-free, or peanut-free. I don't need little pixies or faire folk waving their magic wands over my food before I eat it. I don't pray over my food. Food is food. If you ask me (which you did—ha ha) anyone who needs to fiddle with their food that much is suffering from low self-esteem.

28. No preference. I was raised Catholic, but converted to Judaism when I married Herbert. If I go to church now, it's Mormon. They have the best potlucks.

29. As my granddaughter Chelsea says—Bite Me. She's the brilliant one in the family—unlike Dilbert. (She takes after me).

30. This is a stupid question. We all know that if I could really do anything in the world, I wouldn't be sitting here answering these questions. I'd be fifty years younger with

Marilyn Monroe's curves, Ginger Rogers's legs, Margaret Thatcher's brains, and the passion of Frida. I'd be a patchwork of great women.

31. Ha. Don't you wish.

32. Yes. I had all the paperwork done by my son-in-law who's an attorney. I want to be cremated like Frida. They say her dead body sat straight up in the incinerator, her hair a wild halo of fire. If only I could burn like that—then I'd know I had really lived.

Neighbors

Our mornings—coffee, toast, a wave from his kitchen
to mine. Houses so close I answer my phone when
his rings. White Cockatoo, gift from his ex, shrieks
like a woman being murdered. This morning, a brunette
cooks breakfast, moves in boxes, armloads of clothes,
tosses a Frisbee to her son who chases their dog
through my tulips, breaks a branch off my neighbor's
snowball tree. She builds a rock garden for thyme,
oregano, mint. Mornings, she smokes on the porch.
Bird's moved out.

She knocks on my door for sugar, says she's making
her son's favorite cookies. "He likes Frisbee," I say.
She drags on a Camel, "No—not him. His twin.
Inoperable brain tumor. Come on." She leads me
to her van, points to the dash—a sticker for each
treatment. Fingers flutter over stars, sun, moon,
Mickey. Each a story: chemo, radiation,
experimental pills, hair loss, organ loss—
nine months camped in the hospital parking lot.
I walk her home, the snowball tree heavy with buds.

July 4th. She bundles the sick twin in a Ninja sleeping
bag, props him against the snowball tree. His brother
sets off firecrackers, chases the dog, shakes the tree,
rains white petals over his twin. They play this way
all summer—one resting against the tree, the other
non-stop comedy. Then Disneyland from Make-a-Wish.
They return with stories—roller coasters, boat rides,
Mickey and his gang. The burial is family only.
His mother chain-smokes on the porch, flicks ashes
into thyme. The snowball tree sheds its leaves.
I think it will never stop.

The Tide
For Ethel, 1905-1986

Her grandson rides the bulldozer
like a bronco, bucking earth,
decapitating pine and fir, scattering
sawdust over her house like confetti.

Inside, she drifts among beach glass,
clam shells, sand dollars, old newspapers,
reads yellowed letters to her dog,
Freckles, blind with age.

From her driftwood chair, she overlooks Dogfish Bay
and the boatshed her son built before he died—
millionaire at 40, heart failure at 45—
beach rocks glued like colored moons to the seawall.

She gathers them as they fall, surfaces
polished by the salty tide. She lays them
in the woods where he once hunted wild rabbit,
where old stones glow like fireflies.

Grandfather Howey
1913-1980

A male nurse changes your diaper, ties
your arms to the bedrail, attaches electrodes
to your scalp as he whistles "Yellow Submarine."
Even after 20 years, you still curse their white coats.

The doctor flips the switch. Your hands grip the rail.
Your body jerks and stiffens like the steelhead
you caught that Memorial Day weekend—scales
big as thumbnails, belly soft as morning light.

You remember the day you took your daughter
to Lake Shasta. She holds a string of trout—
her eyes lit like the 4th of July at Balboa Island,
or campfires in the Great Forest. Your wife stands

stiffly by redwoods, your boys wrestle, covered
with leaves and grass. The doctor smiles
as you bite down to kiss your wife goodnight—
the smell of burning lilacs in her hair.

This Late Day

For Grandma Edna
December 6, 1914 - May 6, 2001

She sits on the back porch
shelling peas with slow hands—
liver spots like brown moths.
We watch a summer sun slide

toward the Olympics,
sky pink and hazy as a mirage.
She smiles and says,
I miss the good old days.

What do you miss? I ask.
I miss gettin' up at three in the mornin'
doin' the wash, old board in the tub,
cookin' breakfast for my boys.

She sets the bowl under her chair,
drags pruned branches to the burn pile,
her 85-year-old body ripe
with the cancer that will end her life.

Words unspoken tumble into the fire,
spark and rise like mad dragonflies.
We lift our faces in time to see the sun
light the horizon—

how it burns brightest
just before the end.

Meeting My Friend Jane for the First Time

Before she can offer tea or coffee,
or hopefully some of those macaroons
she's famous for, she shows me the tumor
doctors took out when her daughter was born.
It was bigger than the afterbirth, she brags,
the picture doesn't do it justice. She shoves
the Polaroid closer—*See, See.* I see
a mass of glutinous flesh, dark and wet,
like in the movie "The Blob" when it oozes
under doors, hungers after humans. *See here,*
she points to a spot I can't make out:
this is where it connects—two grown together.
Only a crazy person, I think, could flash
pictures of twin tumors as if they were
her children. But who knows—
maybe if I'd carried them nine months,
nourished them with my nectar, birthed
them alongside my child, I might feel the same.
Maybe after giving birth to death,
you don't care what people think.
You want to see who your friends are,
show them your insides, what you are capable of—
see which ones stay for macaroons.

Like Lemons

She lies beneath a flowered sheet, bed-
bound, broken spine. My hands run the tide
of her body, feel where energy stops, becomes

sticky or dense. I pause above her heart
and a blonde boy appears. He watches
from a golden rowboat, oars still.

My hands weave figure eights, dip
below the surface for life from another place.
I don't mention the boy—how he shimmers

or glows. This cannot be her son.
The month before, I'd met her twin girls,
gone for years now—diseases of heart and spine.

But this boy won't leave. He dips his oars
and motions for me to tell her what I see. Words
like lemons fall from my lips. She closes her eyes,

describes his stillbirth—her cord a noose
around his neck. Heartbreak surfaces
after thirty years. He stays until her tears dry.

Then oars up, boat adrift, eyes
like twin suns, he glides across the water,
oars trailing rings.

For Erica, The Dahlia Fairy

She sings Moody Blues at the office,
rearranges her desk 3 times a week,
her brown flip 10 times a day.

Flirts outrageously—
17 going on 42
going on 9.

She recites her past like a recipe:
latch key kid at 6, dad's biker parties,
hypodermics, insomnia.

Knows more about Jerry Garcia
than I do. Takes me to places I've never been—
tonight, the dahlia farm.

Row after row—Autumn Blaze, Gypsy Girl,
Starchild. She inhales imaginary fragrance,
pale skin against emerald leaves.

She blows on a ladybug—picked them
for her dad's pot plants the year they lived
between Bloodymary's and the beet factory.

Spider webs tangle with Lemon
Ripple. I lose her in Spun Silk,
find her in Harvest Moon.

She waves her dahlia wand
like Glenda, the good witch—
blesses me.

By Liberty Bay

In the gnarled arms of a peeling madrona
hangs a white canoe. Carved into the smooth,

pale tree-flesh is a heart and the words
"Neil loves Amanda."

Why a canoe in a tree? Why not a kite
or a bird's nest or a ukulele?

And who drew the heart?
I assume it was Neil professing his love.

But what if she was the carver,
and she put his name on top to show he loves

her more than she he? But what if within the heart
she knows all love is equal—that it doesn't matter

who's on top—whether he slides into her garden
like an anaconda or she devours him

like the carnivorous plant named
after the goddess of love and sex.

No matter. Love and sex are never equal.
The female always comes out on top—

for what other creature can hold
mankind inside her?

Overflow

The ferry horn blares as I nearly miss the boat,
not wanting to leave my bed, or Bukowski's
Flash of Lightning Behind the Mountain

I toss my purse into a booth—
bits of paper, napkins, wrappers
spilling out

Get lettuce, fish, apples,
feta, six lemons

Remember the boy on the ferry—
how he kept jangling his keys,
his uneasy rectitude

Have my son set up instant messenger
before he leaves

Write about taking Dad off life support
what Grandma said
what I told the priest
how long it took
his breath

Meditate/play Lotto

The dream about running
a bookstore in the 1700's,
raw sewage steaming in the street,
a living master dressed as a bum,
his test

Call Susan for lunch at Sawatdy's

What does the White Rose symbolize?
Purity, innocence, death. A secret
sect that tried to overthrow Hitler

His law: "to use up the best that was in him
each day and to trust that more would come"
Tess on Raymond Carver

"Death will come on padded feet
carrying roses in its mouth"
Bukowski's *Cold Summer*

"You've gotta be shitting me,"
man to his girlfriend

When we were 6—
riding Susan's red tricycle off the cliff,
then later that night—pulling thorns,
blood in our bath

"Holding all I used to be sorry about
like the new moon holding water"
The Sound and the Fury

Dancing at *The Underground*
"You're cute as a bug's ear,"
he said, just out of prison.
He didn't score that night

Play scrabble

Each word a carefully mined
diamond

My protagonist—what does she spend
her life in search of?
What gives her meaning?

Say *I love you* every day

The captain foghorns
our arrival. I gather my scraps,
toss them on my way to Exit

The crowd jockeys,
waiting for the bell

A man coughs,
the jaunty angle of his cigarette

Sylvia

I could have hung myself from the beam
in our old barn, could have let the sway
and swing sing me into that next world.
Could have pressed a gun to my temple.

Could have driven off a cliff or jumped
into the Charles River. I could have swallowed
a bottle of pills—oh, wait—I did,
but only earned three days' oblivion.

I could have opened a vein. Instead, I stuck my head
in an oven and breathed. Why an oven?
Wasn't it awkward—that door jamming my ribs—
that long stretch of my neck?

And what was worth dying for?
I don't remember. I only remember the rush
to dislodge the owl's talons from my heart.
Guess I expected something in that last moment—

I expected a void, or red stars, or a field of white poppies.
I did not expect that death was not the end of sorrow.
I did not expect a longing so intense it left me
roaming the earth like an orphan.

I did not expect to smell lilacs, to taste moonlight,
to hear my beloved whisper love to another woman.
I did not expect to feel regret for all those words
still waiting, patiently, on the tip of my pen.

Ode to Billy Collins' "Litany"

Oh, pretentious poet—to lift
the first two lines of another's poem
and rewrite his ode to one beloved:

"You are the bread and the knife,
the crystal goblet and the wine."
But what if you, dear poet, are really

the bread, the knife, the goblet, the wine?
What if we all are—body and blood,
instrument and vessel?

What if you are the rituals
of each new day? You might also be
the lightly falling snow, the cold wind,

the chickadee composing her canticle.
But not the cicada—
you are never the cicada.

I know you are not the mailman,
nor the lanyard of your youth, and
you are definitely not the potholder.

There's no way you are the dog named Dharma,
or the cat that stretches on its back
like a languid letter "L."

I hope you are not the 300 sheep required
to make a single Guttenberg bible.
But you might be the last meal your wife—

or was it your cat?—cooked for you.
Maybe you're not really the knife, after all.
Maybe, I am the knife. Women are usually the knife.

You can be the crystal goblet and the wine
filling us up. I will give you that—
if you will never rewrite my poems.

You can also be the wooden-strike-anywhere
matches and the pyromaniac mouse
that will set us on fire.

In fact, favorite poet, you can be anything—
as long as you are always the poem
filling us with your words.

Road to Hana, Hawaii

On this snake-like road to hell, I make you stop
twice so I can vomit. White crosses at every curve,
marking those who didn't make it to Seven

Sacred Pools—Oheo Gulch to the locals.
We eat lunch on the banks of Infinity pool:
Cokes and Spam sushi from the local AM/PM.

Afterwards, we hike to the beach, fall asleep
on black sand. I dream of lost ones spinning
around life's curves, crashing into lava walls.

We startle awake to a woman's laugh.
A man chases her, splashes her back. Naked,
they don't see us. We watch their long kiss,

how she maneuvers her legs like a crab
around his waist as the surf lifts them—
her breasts riding the sea.

We hold our breath
for the next big wave,
the one that will sweep them away.

Tourists

Las Caletas, Mexico

By private boat we reach the secret cove—
where palm trees give leafy shade to lovers
hiding away from the world. We move
from jungle's edge to swim under

cerulean water, then fashion a bed
under blue bamboo, under so many stars.
Turtles mate on rocks below and red
macaws call out above. We gaze through bars

of banyon, ginger, palm, and tangled vines.
Trapped by gravity's sweet pull of earth,
like those who've come before, we look for signs—
a shooting star, a universe giving birth.

Like all life's tourists, we want to know
what we are meant to do before we go.

II

Lucky Jacks

I sung of Chaos and Eternal Night,
Taught by the heav'nly Muse to venture down
The dark descent, and up to reascend...

John Milton, "Paradise Lost"

Lucky Jacks

The doctor's words fall like dominos—
suppositions and maybes presented as fact.
His roiling curses wake me

five, six, nine times a night as rain
pounds my window, roots for a way in.
Six days of rain, then sun on the seventh,

that holy day where God rested from the world
and everything in it. In my garden, apple trees
blossom, lilies and lavender strain skyward.

The neighbor's son shrieks, chases his
golden lab. A Boeing 747 scorches sky. But even
lawnmowers and weedwackers can't dim

the song of a blue jay or starlings in the holly tree
that squabble like my grandmother and great aunts
drinking beer and playing a game of Lucky Jacks.

The winter I lie dying

our neighbor brings a gift
of lamb for dinner.
Red juice pools on my plate.

Meat heavy inside me,
I wake to a blood moon,
heart in my ears like hoofbeats,

pupils dilated, tongue thick
and white, skin afire
as if I've been running

my entire life
from the butcher's blade
through fields of yellow

yarrow, sheep's sorrel,
pausing to eat or to play,
to offer my warm wool

to the small hands of the butcher's
boy. He cries when I'm brought
to the dark-stained block

in the shed at the edge
of the field. A blood moon
drips on stone floor.

My last cry echoes
through a winter sky—
all this heavy inside me.

I dream awake,

struggle to sit up,
gaze through blinds
that overlook the marina.
Bars of shadow and light

fall over my sick
bed. Slumber,
like a drug,
leaves me thirsty.

House quiet. Time enough
to consider how life unravels
too fast like a spool
of thread across the floor.

Beyond the blinds
a hawk wraps talons
around deck rail. A leather
cord dangles from his leg

as if he's escaped.
One milky eye stares at me.
Wind stirs his feathers, my sheets,
lifts us above water, boats, mountains.

Black birds caw and chase
but we climb faster, higher,
while they fall back to earth
like clumps of dirt.

We fly beyond sun, moon,
red stars, before words and birth,
into blackness so empty
I feel alive.

In the time it takes a feather
to fall to earth, we're back—
hawk on deck rail,
me in bed. Wings unfold

as he lowers his head
to offer a red berry.
In my mind, I take the gift
and swallow.

His ghost eye watches me
drift under a bed of feathers,
broken tether knocking
against the rail.

In the Ambulance

I lie in deep grass
under a tree of yellow cherries

sweet air of hibiscus
makes me sleepy

a canopy of faces
red lights paint the sky

my heart stops
a stranger leans in

lips sweet
as yellow cherries

Casa de Estrellas
House of Stars, Mexico

No, gracias, I say. *No cerveza.*
Si, si. Tiene cerveza, the old man says,
sliding a frosty glass across the table.
I should take it—celebrate escape
from waiting rooms, from tests, from mountains
of pills, from misdiagnoses. But I read omens
in the lopsided ceiling fan, in a spider's web,
in an old man with one eye. *No, gracias.*
No bebe cerveza, I repeat. How to say
I'm allergic? I hold my palms to my throat.

The wife fires Spanish at her husband.
The smoke-filled room settles. Even the flies
stop their fuss. *Lo siento, Senora,* he says.
No problemo, I say, raising my water glass.
He serves me enchiladas en mole—death
by chocolate. Chases a skinny pit bull
off the porch. After dinner, he offers
a woven palm—green cross of suffering.
In broken English, he says:
free for the dying.

Perfect

The transplanted lilac died
though I watered it,
gave it plant food and lime.

Maybe the lime killed it—
association with bodies,
with graves. Or maybe

I gave it too much water,
too much care. It's always one
or the other. Too much or not enough.

It's never perfect. Unless,
of course, we're talking
about death.

After *The Late, Late Show*

I fall asleep reading Bukowski's
Blue Beads and Bones—
dream I'm buried alive,
crocuses overhead,
roots sucking bones
soft as baby's skin.
I shift. Bukowski
slides off my breast,
snaps shut as if to say
enough.

Pacific Northwest Winter

Twenty-seven days of rain.
Just short of a 53-year record.

Rivers flow over swollen banks.
Garden slugs retreat. I sit cross-legged

in front of my giant SAD light, stare
into white, pray away gray, listen

for life—the splashing,
tapping, rolling,

whooshing
in my veins.

The Art of Flow

The Feng Shui practitioner suggests I place
live fish or a fountain in my entryway

to stimulate chi and bring good luck.
I tell her that my fish tend to die.

She says to put 3—or is it 9—plants
in my bedroom for intimacy. I tell her I have

the same luck with plants I have with fish.
She tries to teach me Kua numbers, the five elements,

my lucky direction. She asks if I can handle
a compass. "No," I say, "but I can tell left from right

and up from down." She walks outside to smoke,
to look up at the stars, at the moon,

at the cavernous black sky. "Not everyone is
meant to be lucky," I say.

"Maybe some of us need to be unlucky
to balance out the energy."

I want to tell her that I can write poems—
that I can arrange words like stones

in a river—syllables that swell into images,
rushing from simile to metaphor,

spiraling like a song stuck in my head,
like a star riding the wind.

III

A New Vocabulary

Come away, O human child!
To the waters and the wild
With a faery, hand in hand,
For the world's more full of weeping
than you can understand.

W.B. Yeats, from "The Stolen Child"

Photograph of My Mother
Whittier, California, 1963

You stand on gray sidewalk. No cracks.
No place for weeds to grow. This California
lawn, short and green. Behind you,
white curtains, a picket fence.

Sun glints off your butterfly glasses,
a golden purse dangles from your wrist.
Your hands rest on your belly.
Do they feel me kick against your walls?

Push your spine straight?
Fight against the life we will live
once we leave this bright place?
You squint into the sun, wait

for your husband to take your picture.
Even now, his shadow looms
in the lower left corner of the Polaroid,
arms lifted like broken wings.

A New Vocabulary

By the time I turn 10
I memorize my father's
words—bimbo, beaver, bitch
witch, gap, gash, hag, bag,

box, floozy, flytrap,
fur bag, tramp, trash,
pant hamster, pussy,
white meat, lesbian, mount,

mule, hoebag, hooker—and more.
Before I even know the meaning
of coitus, copulation, or coition,
I can name the women who do it.

At 4th-grade open house
Ms. Page asks if my father has been
in the war. She says some men come
home from war with a new vocabulary.

I don't know what war she means.
When I say he's always talked that way
she coughs and adjusts her yellow silk
scarf to cover the hickey on her neck.

I want to ask about her purple bloom,
the perfect tooth mark on its edge,
but worry she'll think I'm too forward—
a Jezebel, a strumpet, or a whore.

Green Fruit

My mother would never speak the names of
body parts or tell me how bodies functioned—no
periods or hemorrhoids or penises in our house.
Dad, drunk on screwdrivers, called her frigid.
I looked up the word in our dictionary: *cold,*
without warmth or feeling, lacking emotions. But he
never heard her talk about avocados. When she
was sad or lonely or wanted to feel better she'd
tell me about the avocado tree in her family's
backyard in California. How she'd climb the tree,
higher than her brothers, lie on a thick branch
and choose an avocado to watch over, willing it
to grow and ripen. When it was time, she'd pick
the fruit, hold it in cupped hands as if praying,
then, with just the pressure of her thumbnail,
slice through nippled skin to the soft flesh inside.
Never using a spoon, she'd lift the oval fruit to her
lips, sink teeth into meat, pull green creaminess
into her mouth, hold it there, like a wafer melting
across her tongue.

Prayers for Father

I prayed that cancer would lodge
in your brain. A tumor pressing
on your frontal lobe causing that stutter
and slur of words you uttered each evening,
 "bitch" and "whore" becoming beach and oar—
waves to wash me away from you.

I prayed that lightning would strike
you dead, halve your body like a giant
oak standing solitary and exposed—
electricity lighting your brain, synapses
severed, leaving you wordless and blind.

I prayed you would be flattened by a semi,
strangled by an ex-lover, shot during a drug
deal gone bad, poisoned as you poisoned
the neighbor's dog, buried alive as you buried
us with your brick-heavy words.

On the anniversary of your death, I give thanks
my prayers were never answered, that you died
a "natural" death at fifty-six as your organs shut down:
liver, pancreas, then heart—in that order—as if death
were a systematic march into oblivion, with me left
to write poems instead of prayers.

Last Dance
for Father

Sitting in my third story,
I stare out the open window,
try to write again
of your death—

dandelion skin, bloated limbs
like tree trunks, scent
of butterscotch, your ragged
breath calling back time.

Before me, a brown leaf
rises, swirls, then dips
on an invisible stage.
I reach out to feel

its dry crackling against
my fingers. Too late.
My fist is full
of nothing.

Winter Sky

for Mom

We listen to stars, to the creak of your porch swing.
News of your imminent death, still fresh, curls

around us with misty claws, the doctor's words
groping a way in. Shadows flit across the night—

pieces of you flying away from me. Wind chimes
toll under a cold constellation

as Artemis sings to her lover, Orion. Too late
to save him from burial

in the winter sky, she lights
the moon for him each night. Tonight,

fruit bats dart in and out of the holly tree,
screech: *hurry, hurry, hurry.*

On Fjord Drive

the retired Wonder Bread driver
idles his mower as I walk by.
"Nice day isn't it," he hollers.
I stop, not sure how I came so far.

"How's your mom doing?" he yells over
rosebushes. I say she's fine, considering.
I test how much he wants:
"She's at the nursing home now.

Doesn't really remember anybody."
He nods, looks down at yellow buds,
snaps his head up. "Well, tell her I said hello.
Gotta get back to work. You know how it is."

He puts the mower in gear. His wife peers
through bamboo blinds, drops
them, as if I were contagious—
the blinds swing wildly in agreement.

Positano, Italy
Poulsbo, Washington

White-haired signora passes
as I huff up Via Marconi, bags
of groceries hung from my arms like bloated
water wings

My mother never learned to swim but sank
like stone. The nursing home attendant takes care
not to get water in her eyes

Sea salt dusts our dinner: fettuccini with pesto,
mozzerella, bread, tomatoes from the market. Red wine
stains the tablecloth—our offering above
a star-ridden sea

She's spoon-fed mashed potatoes, peas,
milk thickened with gelatin, all easy to swallow—
that small act a hazard now

Carefully, we hike a castle's dry moat, visit
cathedrals, cemeteries, Crypt of Skulls.
Everywhere we turn, Bernini's
marble ghosts

Once-blue eyes glaze over. Shadows flicker
across her screen—*Days of Our Lives,*
The Price is Right—no more

In Italy, even the stairs are old. Steps of stone,
of petrified wood, go on forever. Muscles
afire, feet blistered,
we climb

"Sooner or later she'll forget how to swallow.
When this happens, do you want tube feeding
or just water?" Doesn't take long to choose

Water, the element Bernini harnessed
best, how it swirls and eddies
around the river god's stone hips,
              buoys him up.

Prayer for Mother

Om Namah Guru
Om Namah Shivaya [1]

Hallowed be her name on heavenly lips,
give her her daily bread,
let thy kingdom come
for she who lives between worlds—
not here, nor there.

Her mind—
dark and graceful wilderness
curls in on itself,
hands wrapped in gauze
like a newborn.

Body tis of thee—earth to ashes
O, God of love and release,
Oh Lord, Giver of Life,
Dispeller of Miseries—
hear my prayer.

Baptize her with your blood,
release her from life unremembered—
nights tossed onto the street like a beggar,
days hiding bruises, neighbors like blind men,
heart ripped out like a weed.

Blessed is she among women
while I—fruit of her womb—write
poems on her bones. To the one
who gave me life, leave me
now on wings of light.

Patti Dana
Patti Dana[2]

O, Lord, hear my prayer.

[1] Om Namah Shivaya is a Hindu mantra meaning "I bow to Shiva."
Shiva is the supreme reality, the inner Self. It is the name given to
consciousness that dwells in all.
[2] Patti Dana is a Buddhist chant that allows the petitioner to transfer merits
(good deeds) to a living or deceased relative.

IV

Lessons

For what is it to die but to stand naked
in the wind and to melt into the sun?
Only when you drink from the river
of silence shall you indeed sing.
And when you have reached the mountain
top, then you shall begin to climb.
And when the earth shall claim your limbs,
then shall you truly dance.

Kahil Gibran, from "On Death"

You teach me how to walk

around this island's 150 acres of forest garden.
Counterclockwise, we step along the gravel path
through thigh-high grass, through pine, cedar, spruce.

You teach me to walk lightly so swallows won't
dive-bomb to protect their young. You teach me
to stop and listen to their chorus.

You teach me not to stumble over roots,
or imaginary ghosts as we walk through a tunnel
of green to a lily pond edged by marsh grass.

You teach me to listen as the white swan glides
across glass, to laugh at a brace of ducks splashing
and gargling under water-logged branches.

You teach me to be gentle as the breeze stirring
a dragonfly to light on the back of my hand—
to contemplate her iridescence, her certitude.

You teach me to see dragons in the sky—
clouds spewing fire at the sun. You teach me
to love you in stillness and un-stillness,
to be the dragon and the dragonfly.

New Year's Eve, 2014

Sitting by the window, I scribble my last lines of the year.
Fireworks echo across the bay. Blackbirds ruffle feathers,
shift their weight from foot to foot in naked alder.
Do they sense the passage of time?
Worry about getting old or falling apart?

When this poem is finished, we'll soak under a canopy
of stars so old some no longer exist, our eyes the first
to see their light. Our voices rising over Jacuzzi jets
and bubbles—will we talk about our year?
Will we dare mention the future?

And how should we celebrate? Champagne? You're not
supposed to have sugar. Grapes? I'd peel them for you but
you've had the hiccups for 96 hours. Scatter rose petals
across the water like the night we spoke our vows?

Or would the petals reveal my fear this might be our last
New Year's? Our last soak? Our last kiss?
Will these last lines reveal answers?
And, if not answers, at least comfort? Words and lines
and stanzas and even spaces,   especially spaces—

what are they, if not for comfort? My heart in black
and white, or sometimes purple, or blue like a bruise
blossoming over my pages. Time. Moves. Too. Quickly.
If only I could slow it down with punctuation or white
space.

"Three months," said the doctor. Impressed with the
smooth, unwavering quality of his voice, I forgot what
he said next. You joked around, not wanting him to feel bad.

"If I beat this, doc, will you buy me a steak dinner?
Will I be your prize patient for at least a month?"

"You'd be my prize patient forever." We shook his hand then,
said our thank you's—as if he'd just given us the best news
of the year. Maybe he had—now we could name
the symptoms and fatigue—and didn't a wise man
once say that to know thyself was to know God?

Three months later—New Year's Eve, the breath
between endings and beginnings, the space between
knowing and not knowing. Are we dying to live
or living to die? Do blackbirds fly at night?
Do dead stars ever really go dark?
When I'm done writing, does the poem end?

Rising

I watch you each morning before
the jays jabber their cacophonies
and the cats demand their breakfast.

I look for the rise and fall
of your shoulders as you lie
curled on your side,

my gaze peaceful, not panicked
as in the early days.
Somehow, a deep stillness

has taken root inside me.
Then your ribs rise, lifting
your blankets like the sea

swelling with the tides.
I too rise, careful
not to wake you.

Soaking in sulfur water

stretched out side by side
in cast iron, claw-footed tubs,
we watch dying stars and a snow
moon light the broken grass of winter—
skeleton trees missing leaves
that lie molted on the ground.
Sparks from our fire climb
the sky and turn to ash.

Echolocation

In the Pacific bottlenose dolphins
weave through waves like loose stitches.
Earth's magnetic field steadies
their course. Echolocation tells
them when to outrun the great white,
when to feast on squid or shrimp.

Tonight—rain on salal, moths
at the screen. It hasn't been spring
long enough to forget the silence
of winter. We play a round of Scrabble—
like the days before your diagnosis,
before our words became hard to find.

A bat loops over the pier, its extra sense
guides it through night, through alleys,
through canyons and caves. It loops
once more and is gone, leaving us
to make up truths as if inventing new words,
to feel our way home, one letter at a time.

Chrysalis

Your hiccups lasted 7 weeks—a tumor
pressed against your vagus nerve like
a caterpillar breaking free of its cocoon.

Late at night, I lay on my side, one hand
placed flat on your back—holding you here—
my other hand scribbling words on paper.

I had not written a poem in over a year but
suddenly I couldn't not write—as if each word
the hiccups stole from you poured from my pen.

7 weeks. 18 poems. Then you died and
my words dried up, leaving lakes, rivers,
oceans of longing for the heat of you—

each salted drop one of our lost words—
soundless and silent as the susurrus
of butterfly wings.

Suppose

Suppose when I say *spring*
a butterfly lands on the back
of my hand, fresh from its cocoon.

Suppose when I say *summer*
a dolphin and her calf spin circles
beneath us in Hawaiian waters.

Suppose when I say *fall*
two eagles circle over us
on unseen currents.

Suppose when I say *winter*
a spider spins its web
for a long hibernation.

Suppose when I say *forever*
you look into my eyes
and say *I'm sorry. I love you.*

Suppose when I touch your cheek,
you take a breath and die.
Suppose this is enough.

The Persistence of Yellow

Mustard. Pollen dust on my fingers.
Black-eyed Susan petals.
Canaries.

Yolk.

A stray cat's straw bed.
Hollandaise sauce. Butter.
Turmeric Tea.

Roses: Michelangelo, amber queen.
My skin after eating too many carrots.

Limoncello.

The yellow jacket that stung me.
Winnie the Pooh. A weathered cocoon.

Honey. Week-old chicks. Scotch broom.
Swallowtail butterflies.

His hair in summer.
His eyes near the end.
The coins we sold to pay for his cremation.

Flames.

Scattering Ashes

Harrison Lake, Canada, August 17, 2015

I stand on the lakeshore, gaze
into its blue and green mirror—
cloudless sky above,
algae blooming below.

Your ashes ride the wind,
dust my skin, bits of white bone
speckle underwater rocks
like stars against black moons.

I pinch flower tops,
toss them into the water
only to have the breeze
blow them back to me.

I scoop them up,
throw them out again,
feeling as if I have
done this before—

this ancient ritual of
letting something go
to have it return.
But you are gone—

dissolved
into the lake bed,
into the water,
into me.

Two blue dragonflies
skim the surface,
laying eggs
over your grave.

A bald eagle swoops
down to catch a fish
that has breathed you
into its gills.

A hawk carves lazy circles

over the bay, higher and higher,
a speck in the wind. He flies into
a void where time meets no time,
where he continues to climb, carrying
me away from a world that has no patience
for grief or for loss—
away from a world that tells me
to move on, to remember only the good,

a world that doesn't want to know
I still write you love letters,
a world that doesn't want to know
I still hear your voice telling me
the womb is the grave
and the grave is the womb.

A world that doesn't want to know
I have tasted your bones,
I have held your ash in my mouth,
I have rubbed you into my skin.

Suppose someday I say hot springs

will I remember our hike up Sol Duc,
how we riffed fingers over silk moss,
how we stepped stone to stone
over the creek that crossed our path,
how we posed for a photo on the rickety
footbridge under fir and red cedar?

Will I remember Harrison's five pools, our walk
to the source where earth exhaled sulfur
and squished beneath our feet? Will I remember
the Black Forest restaurant and those schnitzels:
cordon bleu, shrimp, mushroom—*too mushroomy,*
you said—and plain—*too plain,* I said?

Will I remember Bonneville—
private hot tub on our balcony, foxes slinking
from low-lying hills, hours by the stone fireplace—
you reading articles on quantum science,
me writing poems in a notebook—
both making up stories about strangers?

What if I forget it all—forest, foxes, food, stories?
Will reading these words push back time
like a branch across our trail, letting me run
my hand along the soft hair of your arms,
lay my head on your shoulder one more time,
inhale your scent like the sun?

Sun on Mud Flats

We wrinkle our noses, walk past the marina
to this small park where my grandparents strung

oyster shells for extra money, old clam shed
now replaced by concrete and by picnic benches.

Couples, heads bent, jab at their smart phones.
We hold hands, watch two eagles circle above

then swoop down to the sea, claws extended
to a line of ducklings following their mother.

We yell. We try to wave them off. The ducklings bob
under water, swim to safety beneath the pier.

To the couples with bent heads, I want to shout *Look up!*
Over the next 10 years, these words become ours.

When you die, a grief like late winter fog settles in.
Then one day, I hear a voice—*Look up!*

Outside my window an eagle, wings lifted
in wind, stares at me.

Later that night at the beach, our pregnant daughter-in-law,
blonde hair flying in wind, points and yells, *Look up!*

Above our heads, an eagle spirals higher, higher.
I watch until my neck aches, until there is only sky.

Lessons

You taught meditation. You taught Qi Gong.
You said I was your best student—
second woman to complete 105 days
of Iron Stomach, that hour-long exercise
of breath and animal poses. I became
eagle, rabbit, tiger.

You taught me how to let go of fear,
how to cry, how to talk dirty in bed,
how to love a wizard who believed
even a small-town girl could be somebody.

I taught you imperfection could be perfection—
failure to learn piano meant you were born to sing.
I taught you unconditional love is real—
harsh words born of fatigue and illness
could not push me away.

We learned magic is real, even mischievous—
the time pickled mushrooms appeared in our cart
in a store that didn't sell pickled anything,
the time you entered one elevator, then walked
out another on the opposite side of the hotel.

After your death, the lessons continue—
I tell you how I miss your body next to mine,
how even the cats grieve, how they hide when I cry.
I tell you I've learned new ways to cry—loud
like an animal—a sound that really does heal.

You teach me you are still here.
No barriers or body to stop you,

you wrap me in a thousand suns.
Early mornings, late nights—
those times when the world is still—
I feel you. I hear you. I ask for signs.

You send me dragonflies and snow.
In dreams, we walk hand in hand
through white poppies.
We sit in the sky
in a circle of shamans who allow me
to ask one question.
But each time I speak,
they shake their heads.
They tell me
I already know the answers.

First Year

To be pushed off a cliff 100 times a day—
no warning, free-falling into nothingness,
no place to land since someone's stolen the ground.

To be plunked into a rollercoaster, dragged
to the highest peak, then dropped far underground
where I lie motionless, hoping no one sees me.

To be a clock out of time—
to rise, work, eat, try to sleep, then repeat.
Each day, the day you died.

To be a broken mirror—to smile, to practice my laugh
until someone asks how I am and my voice splits
like static between radio stations.

To be a square, three-legged table bracing
for something light as a pencil
or heavy as a poem.

What People Talk About When They Talk About Death

Time heals all wounds.
Bullshit. Nothing heals death.

You'll get over it.
F-you. What if I don't want to?

When you're ready to start dating again…
After two weeks you say this?
Never in a million years with you.

Why didn't you tell me he was sick. I could have saved him.
Sorry. Didn't realize you were Jesus Christ.

You don't need his pistol, do you?
Yes, I do. To protect myself from dumb-asses like you.

Focus on what you're grateful for.
I'm grateful I kept his pistol for dumb-asses like you.

At least you have your memories.
At least, they won't include you.

Grief must be teaching you something you need to learn.
Great! Let me teach you something…
come a little closer.

You're smiling! I'm glad you're doing so well.
This is my mask. Did you look into my eyes?

He was so young.
Yeah, and you're not. Why are you still here?

He lived a full life.
What does this mean? That he did everything he wanted?
That he was ready to go? Not even close.

I can't be around you. It's too painful.
I wish I could leave myself too.

Why did he die?
Silence.

And then there are those who say nothing.

Valentines

And these are my loves: red wine, orange cats,
the smell of clove cigarettes, Leonard Cohen's gravely
voice, words like sibilate and firefly
and lovely and valium,
rain like pebbles on our sunroom roof,
or hail the size of Easter eggs,
church bells in the morning, cradling my guitar
like a tired friend,
leaning into corners on my motorcycle,
the way you brag about my writing to friends
and strangers,
your unquenchable thirst
for life and laughter and your hunger that isn't hunger
but a life reaching back for itself, and how
we say *I love you, I love you more, I love you most,*
singing too loudly,
swimming in the ocean,
warm water like lips sliding over my skin,
the water in me searching for the water not in me,
your mouth eroding my edges
like sand consuming
the tides.

Folding Laundry

Tossing an armful of warm towels
onto the living room couch
I contemplate the difference
between sorrow and loss.
I tell our 3 cats I am grateful
for the love they showed you,
for the days, weeks, months
they took turns on your lap.
They knead the pile of laundry,
seeking warmth,
seeking a place to sleep.
As I fold the last towel,
they accuse me with their eyes,
as if I don't understand.

Night Driving

The deer stops in the middle
of a back country road.
Tri-tone brown, ears
like antennae, she stands
still, almost regal.
Her red eyes stare into mine
as if to ask where I am going.
I tell her I don't know.
I say the words out loud
and wait.

All This Blue

At the casino hotel, I set up my computer
near the stone fireplace while you arrange
candles on the mantel, tease the barkeep
over club soda and bitters.

At Barnes and Noble, I finger pages
of new fiction while you devour books
on everything from Android apps
to Taoist secrets of love.

At the coffee shop, I scribble poems
about endings, not realizing these words
are the start of a long grief, while you read
quantum physics and chat with local police
in pressed blue uniforms.

Winters, we eat endless bowls of soup
at the Poulsbohemian Coffeehouse.
Summers, we lounge against Fay Bainbridge
driftwood, watch Salsbury Point fishermen.

After you die, I try go back
to our places. But I cannot find you
in the park, the clouds, or the sea.
I cannot find you in fireplace flames
or at the end of a fishing line.

But I do find you in the coffee shop—
in the calm of police uniforms,
in my words that grow strong again,
that find meaning in this place
where even time lies down
in the midst of all this blue.

V

When Love Comes

Lovers don't finally meet somewhere.
They're in each other all along.

Rumi

Seabeck, Hood Canal

I sit on a rock wall
facing sea and mountains,
journal in my lap,
camera round my neck,
waiting for that time
just before sunset
when clouds part,
when sunfire rains down
on mountains.

A skein of geese soars
above me, pulls apart,
then comes back together
like the part of me that stretches
across the canal.
Here, there are mountains
behind mountains.
I feel the effort it must have taken
to push upward, ascending
to heights unknown.

Second Year

First time I laughed out loud, then looked around
for the person making that raucous noise.

First time I slept through the night and went
an entire day without crying.

First time I shed happy tears,
holding our newborn grandson.

First time I went to the movies by myself—
didn't feel a million eyes staring.

First time I slept in our old bedroom in a new bed
and went 2 days without crying.

First time I visited Seattle's butterfly museum for your
birthday—didn't fall apart—didn't stay in bed for a week.

First time I lived alone in 50 years,
didn't cry 7 days straight.

First time I went hiking in the woods by myself
and was not afraid I'd get lost.

First time I noticed another man's smile
across a crowded coffee shop.

First time I took myself on a dinner date, reading
"A Moveable Feast" over spaghetti and meatballs.

First time I imagined kissing another man,
2-day stubble against my cheek.

First time I said out loud: I want to be here.
I want to fall in love with love.

Butterfly House
Pacific Science Center, Seattle

The sign says tread lightly
because butterflies might land
on the stone path. I understand
their need to rest, to feel something
solid beneath them.

Another sign warns not to touch them—
they can't self-repair damaged wings
but can still fly with missing pieces.

I stand still. A black and orange
monarch lands on my yellow hair.
After 9 months in its chrysalis,
the monarch will only live
a few days to a couple of weeks.

Can it smell my wonder?
Does it sense the butterflies inside me—
a thousand wings quivering for spring,
preparing for new life?
I open my mouth to set them free.

Coffee

Across the coffee shop, I catch you
looking at me. You glance away.
Later, you catch me watching you.

Googling "How to Flirt Over 50,"
I see not much has changed in 30 years
except it says I shouldn't giggle—
giggling is for girls.

When you pass by to get cream,
I practice my throaty laugh
and have a coughing fit.

I practice the article's advice:
Smile. Make eye contact.
Look away. Blush.

My blush triggers a hot flash,
turning my skin candy-apple red,
color of harlots everywhere.

You smile, stir cream into your coffee.
A sparkle in your eye swirls my insides
hot and bitter, silky and sweet.

When Love Comes

When love comes like a morning glory
opening to first light,

when love comes like the blues, plucking
buttercup petals, singing "he loves me,
he loves me not," and places those petals
in my hair like a coronet,

when love comes like a newborn colt's
first awkward steps,

when love comes like the sun
after a month of rain and I lift my face
as if to feel its heat for the first time,

when love comes like an infant
in the night, suckling my breast,
I want to greet it with open eyes
and a smile, saying, "You, again?"

I want to greet it without demanding
promises it can't keep. I want to greet it
brimming with questions—
when love comes

will I be a jackal devouring
each morsel or a honey bee
sampling each flower in the garden?

will it tangle around me
like a forest vine or buoy me
like an ocean current?

will it leave a taste like bitter chocolate,
or like dandelion wine—
sweet and hopeful on my tongue?

When love comes
I don't want to hesitate
or talk myself out of it
or lock my windows
and hide under the bed.

When love comes
I want to say
take me I am yours.

I want to say
let this be the last time.

I want to say
stay with me
until the end.

Acknowledgements

Ars Poetica: A Hawk Carves Lazy Circles, Advice from a Male Tasmanian Cave Spider, Chrysalis, Green Fruit, Liberty Bay, The Persistence of Yellow, You Teach Me How to Walk

Bellowing Ark: For Erica, the Dahlia Fairy

Pacific Northwest Writer's Conference Contest: Grandfather Howey; Positano, Italy/Poulsbo Washington; New Year's Eve; Valentines.

Pitkin Review: Casa de Estrellas, Overflow, Photograph of My Mother.

Surrey International Writers' Conference Contest: Broken Things, Assisted Living Questionnaire.

Writer's Digest Competitions: Butterfly House, I Dream Awake, Prayer for Mother, Valentines.

❖ ❖ ❖

My heartfelt thanks to the following for helping make this book a possibility:

My longtime friend and poetry mentor, Nancy Rekow, without whose love and guidance this book would not have happened, and our Night Writers group, including Everett Thompson and Bob McAllister, for their editorial insights and tough love; Carol J. Bankhead, cover artist, for her friendship, extraordinary talent, and camping expertise; Jos Marlowe for her love, friendship, wisdom, and long literary talks (and everything else too

numerous to recount here); my writing partner, Jana
Bourne, for her love, friendship, writing and editing
acumen, and inspiration to keep reaching for my dreams;
Michael Klein, Amy Liu, Paul Selig, and Goddard
College for providing a stimulating and expansive
environment to pursue my art and for encouraging me
to go deeper within myself; Margie Lawson of the online
Lawson Writers Academy for enriching my prose and
poetry with her incredible teachings; Paula Gill for her
expert book designing skills and guidance; Ars Poetica
artists Bryn Hamano Hughes, Evy Olson Halvorsen,
and Sydni Sterling for transforming my words into
beautiful works of art; my fellow poet and pet sitter
extraordinaire, Ellen Elizabeth, for loving my fur babies
so I could attend writing retreats and conferences to
better my craft; my cousin, Susan Nausid, for her lifelong
love and encouragement—I never would have made it
this far without you. To all my friends who continue to
lift me up and love me unconditionally on a daily basis—
thank you. I love you.

Thank you to my son, Cliff DesPeaux, for his artistic
contribution to this book. And thank you to Cliff, his
beautiful wife, Angie, and my grandson for everything
that gives my life purpose and meaning. Finally, I am
eternally grateful to Dale Fawcett for his love and for
always believing in me. Thank you for being my angel.

In Writing Workshop
For my fellow Night Writers

"I'm not totally against 'ings,' though I'm not sure about
that 'arching curve'—something feels off," says Nancy,
who's wearing, or wears, her new chicken apron
in accordance with Minnie Rose Lovgreen's
raising-chickens-who-teach-you-about-life book theme.

After Celine reads her Guanajuato poem,
Nancy asks, "But what color is the bird?"
Celine says "Teal." I say how I like her gold-embossed
T-shirt from that Mexican town.
Everett says, "Seal? What color is seal?"
Celine thanks me and says sometimes people think
her T-shirt says "Guantanamo." This makes her turn white.
"No, it's teal," shouts Nancy across the room.
"Oh, I thought she said seal," says Everett.

Out of the blue, Nancy asks,
"What do you call those garages they deliver?"
Everett says, "Dumpsters?"
Bob, a builder and a poet, straightens them out—
"No. No. They're pre-fab."
The new girl, Judy, asks if pre-fab is a type of outline.

Bob tells a story told to him about a relative whose baby,
little Dickie, stopped breathing. The relative said, "The doctor
breathed into Dick's mouth and that's where artificial
'semination came from." Everett pipes up that his grandfather
artificially inseminated cows. Nancy says one of her students
wrote a book about inseminating cows.
I say I never realized cows had it so hard.

I read my poem, "After the Diagnosis."
Bob looks at me and says, "You should try some expositories."
I stop and think—didn't I add them to my grocery list
on the refrigerator? But how does Bob know?

Carol Despeaux Fawcett lives in the Pacific Northwest where she grew up. She graduated from Western Washington University and earned her MFA degree from Goddard College. She is an award-winning poet whose work has appeared in many journals. Her memoir and her poetry have won first place in the Pacific Northwest Writer's Contest and her current work-in-progress, a fantasy novel, was a finalist. Her poems have been finalists in the *Writer's Digest* Annual Poetry Competition, the Surrey International Writers' Conference, and Ars Poetica. She received a poetry grant from *Return to Creativity*. *The Dragon and The Dragonfly* is her first book of poetry. She co-writes www.OneWildWord.com, a blog for writers. Learn more about her writing a www.cdfawcett.com. When she's not writing or running her health and wellness business, she enjoys spending time in nature, petting the neighborhood dogs, waiting on her two cats, riding her motorcycle, and pretending she can play guitar. She also manages www.Poulsboairbnb.com

Cliff DesPeaux is a visual media specialist, photographer, Search and Rescue volunteer, drone hobbyist, Pulitzer Prize winner, and former pianist. His photojournalism has appeared in The New York Times, The Seattle Times, The Seattle Post-Intelligencer and been syndicated globally via The Associated Press and Reuters. He resides with his wife, son, two corgis and 30 chickens in Maltby, WA. Get in touch with Cliff at clifford@despeaux.com.

Made in the USA
Columbia, SC
14 December 2017